Creepy Creatures

AYE-AYES

BY TRUDY BECKER

WWW.APEXEDITIONS.COM

Copyright © 2025 by Apex Editions, Mendota Heights, MN 55120. All rights reserved. No part of this book may be reproduced or utilized in any form or by any means without written permission from the publisher.

Apex is distributed by North Star Editions:
sales@northstareditions.com | 888-417-0195

Produced for Apex by Red Line Editorial.

Photographs ©: Shutterstock Images, cover, 1, 4–5, 6, 10–11, 14–15, 16–17, 18–19, 22–23, 24, 25; iStockphoto, 7, 13, 26–27, 29; Nick Garbutt/RGB Ventures/SuperStock/Alamy, 8; John Dambik/Alamy, 12; Joe Blossom/Alamy, 20

Library of Congress Control Number: 2024943571

ISBN
979-8-89250-320-4 (hardcover)
979-8-89250-358-7 (paperback)
979-8-89250-432-4 (ebook pdf)
979-8-89250-396-9 (hosted ebook)

Printed in the United States of America
Mankato, MN
012025

NOTE TO PARENTS AND EDUCATORS
Apex books are designed to build literacy skills in striving readers. Exciting, high-interest content attracts and holds readers' attention. The text is carefully leveled to allow students to achieve success quickly. Additional features, such as bolded glossary words for difficult terms, help build comprehension.

CHAPTER 1
FINDING FOOD 4

CHAPTER 2
BIZARRE BODIES 10

CHAPTER 3
EAT UP 16

CHAPTER 4
LIFE CYCLE 22

COMPREHENSION QUESTIONS • 28
GLOSSARY • 30
TO LEARN MORE • 31
ABOUT THE AUTHOR • 31
INDEX • 32

CHAPTER 1

FINDING FOOD

Night falls in the rainforest. An aye-aye wakes up. He climbs out of his leafy nest and starts searching for food.

Aye-ayes sleep in nests during the day. They come out at night.

Aye-ayes often climb up to 60 feet (18 m) above the ground.

LIFE UP HIGH

Aye-ayes sometimes go down to the ground. But they spend most of their time in trees. They sleep, hunt, and eat high in the branches.

The aye-aye moves through the trees. He spots a rotting branch. The soft wood is falling apart. The aye-aye taps the branch with his long finger.

Aye-ayes eat insects that live inside trees.

The aye-aye listens closely. He hears an insect inside the branch. So, he pokes his finger into a hole in the wood. He pulls out the bug and eats it.

FAST FACT
Aye-ayes have six fingers on each hand. The third finger is extra long and thin.

◀ An aye-aye's third finger is about 3 inches (8 cm) long.

CHAPTER 2

BIZARRE BODIES

Aye-ayes are **lemurs**. They live in Madagascar. Aye-ayes weigh about 4 pounds (1.8 kg). Their bodies are about 15 inches (38 cm) long.

Madagascar is a large island off the coast of Africa. Several kinds of lemurs live there.

Aye-ayes live in forests and **swamps**. They are excellent climbers. Their sharp claws grip branches. And their long, bushy tails help them balance.

An aye-aye's tail is more than 20 inches (50 cm) long.

Much of Madagascar's forests were cut down to make room for farms and homes.

DYING OUT

Humans have destroyed many aye-aye **habitats**. Plus, some people kill the animals. They think aye-ayes bring bad luck. As a result, the animals are **endangered**.

Aye-ayes may scream or puff up their fur to scare other animals.

Aye-ayes are **nocturnal**. Their large, yellow eyes see well in the dark. And their dark fur helps them stay hidden. Aye-ayes also have large ears. They can hear very quiet sounds.

FAST FACT

Aye-ayes have some white hairs. They raise these hairs when scared or excited.

CHAPTER 3

EAT UP

Aye-ayes mainly eat insects and fruit. The animals forage each night. They may travel more than 2 miles (3.2 km) looking for food.

Aye-ayes often eat sweet foods, such as coconuts and bananas.

To find insects, aye-ayes tap on trees. Then they listen. They can tell if branches have holes or tunnels made by bugs. They can also hear bugs moving around inside.

LONG FINGERS

An aye-aye's extra-long finger connects to a special joint. The joint lets the finger move in any direction. The finger can **rotate**. It can also bend backwards.

Aye-ayes tap branches very quickly. The sounds cause bugs to move.

When they find insects, aye-ayes often chew holes in branches. Then they reach their long fingers inside. Their curved claws scrape out the food.

FAST FACT

An aye-aye's front teeth can chew through concrete.

◀ An aye-aye's front teeth never stop growing.

CHAPTER 4

LIFE CYCLE

Aye-ayes spend most of their time alone. They mark their **territories** with smells. However, they sometimes share nests. And they come together to **mate**.

Female aye-ayes find males to mate with every two to three years.

Newborn aye-ayes weigh 3 to 5 ounces (85 to 140 g).

About five months after mating, female aye-ayes give birth. Each female has one baby. She takes care of the baby alone.

STAYING SAFE

Aye-ayes build nests high in trees. These nests are made of leaves and twigs. Females give birth in the nests. For two months, the babies remain inside. This helps them stay safe from **predators**.

Fossas are catlike animals. They sometimes hunt aye-ayes.

At first, babies are tiny and helpless. They slowly learn to climb and find food. After about two years, aye-ayes are fully grown. They go live on their own.

FAST FACT
Aye-ayes may live for about 20 years in the wild.

Baby aye-ayes climb slowly at first. Over time, they learn how to move fast.

COMPREHENSION QUESTIONS

Write your answers on a separate piece of paper.

1. Write a few sentences explaining how aye-ayes use their long fingers.

2. What part of an aye-aye's body do you think is the creepiest? Why?

3. How long do baby aye-ayes stay in their nests?
    - A. two months
    - B. five months
    - C. two years

4. At what age do aye-ayes leave their mothers?
    - A. five months old
    - B. two years old
    - C. 20 years old

5. What does **grip** mean in this book?

Aye-ayes live in forests and swamps. They are excellent climbers. Their sharp claws grip branches.

    A. to snap and break
    B. to fall off
    C. to grab and hold

6. What does **forage** mean in this book?

The animals forage each night. They may travel more than 2 miles (3.2 km) looking for food.

    A. to sleep in trees
    B. to search for food
    C. to care for babies

Answer key on page 32.

GLOSSARY

endangered
In danger of dying out forever.

habitats
The places where animals normally live.

lemurs
Types of animals that live in trees and have long, furry tails.

mate
To form a pair and come together to have babies.

nocturnal
Awake and active at night.

predators
Animals that hunt and eat other animals.

rotate
To turn around or move in a circle.

swamps
Areas of low land covered in water, often with many plants.

territories
Areas that animals live in and defend.

BOOKS

Bassier, Emma. *Aye-Ayes*. Minneapolis: Abdo Publishing, 2020.

Doeden, Matt. *Travel to Madagascar*. Minneapolis: Lerner Publications, 2024.

Wilson, Libby. *Mind-Boggling Mammals*. Mendota Heights, MN: Apex Editions, 2024.

ONLINE RESOURCES

Visit **www.apexeditions.com** to find links and resources related to this title.

ABOUT THE AUTHOR

Trudy Becker lives in Minneapolis, Minnesota. She likes exploring new places and loves anything involving books.

INDEX

B
babies, 24–26

C
claws, 12, 21

E
ears, 15
eyes, 15

F
fingers, 7, 9, 18, 21
food, 4, 16, 21, 26
fur, 15

H
habitats, 13

I
insects, 9, 16, 18, 21

L
lemurs, 10

M
Madagascar, 10
mating, 22, 24

N
nests, 4, 22, 25
nocturnal, 15

P
predators, 25

S
swamps, 12

T
tails, 12
teeth, 21

ANSWER KEY:
1. Answers will vary; 2. Answers will vary; 3. A; 4. B; 5. C; 6. B